Start TO Finish
Second Series

Everyday Products

FROM Wax TO Crayon

● ROBIN NELSON

LERNER PUBLICATIONS COMPANY › Minneapolis

Lerner Publications Company
A division of Lerner Publishing Group, Inc.
241 First Avenue North
Minneapolis, MN 55401 U.S.A.

Website address: www.lernerbooks.com

Photo Acknowledgments
The images in this book are used with the permission of: AP Photo/Steve Klaver, pp. 1, 9, 11; © Svitlana Kataieva/Shutterstock.com, p. 3; © Philip Scalia/Alamy, p. 5; © William Thomas Cain/Stringer/Getty Images, pp. 7, 17, 19; A36609 Daniel Karmann Deutsch Presse Agentur/Newscom, p. 13; AP Photo/Rick Smith, p. 15; © Robert Pernell/Shutterstock.com, p. 21; © Digital Vision/Getty Images, p. 23.

Front cover: © Peter Morley/Shutterstock.com.

Main body text set in Arta Std Book 20/26.
Typeface provided by International Typeface Corp.

Library of Congress Cataloging-in-Publication Data

Nelson, Robin, 1971–
        From wax to crayon / by Robin Nelson.
            p.   cm. — (Start to finish, second series.
        Everyday products)
        Audience: Grades K to 3.
        Includes index.
        ISBN 978–0–7613–9183–8 (lib. bdg. : alk. paper)
        1. Crayons—Juvenile literature. 2. Wax-modeling—Juvenile literature. I. Title.
TS1268.N45 2013
665'.4—dc23   2012007923

Manufactured in the United States of America
1 – MG – 12/31/12

TABLE OF Contents

I color with crayons. How are they made?

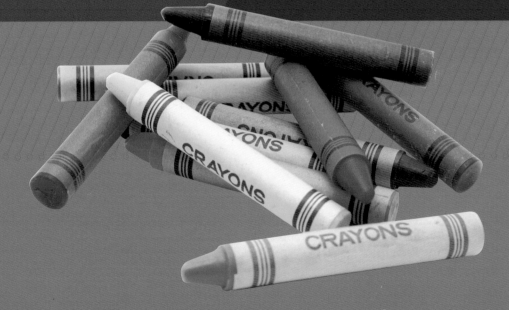

Wax melts.

Crayons start as clear wax. Wax is made into crayons at a **factory**. Large tanks heat the wax. The wax melts into a gooey liquid.

A worker adds color.

Pipes carry the clear wax into many pots called **vats**. A worker adds colored powder called **pigment** to the vats. A different color is stirred into each vat.

The wax is shaped.

The colored wax is poured into a **mold**. The mold has many holes. Each hole is shaped like a crayon. The wax fills the holes.

The wax gets hard.

Cold water flows under the mold. It cools the wax. Cooling makes the wax hard. The wax becomes crayons.

A worker checks the crayons.

The crayons are taken out of the mold.
A worker checks each crayon for chips
or dents. Crayons with chips or dents
will be melted and molded again.

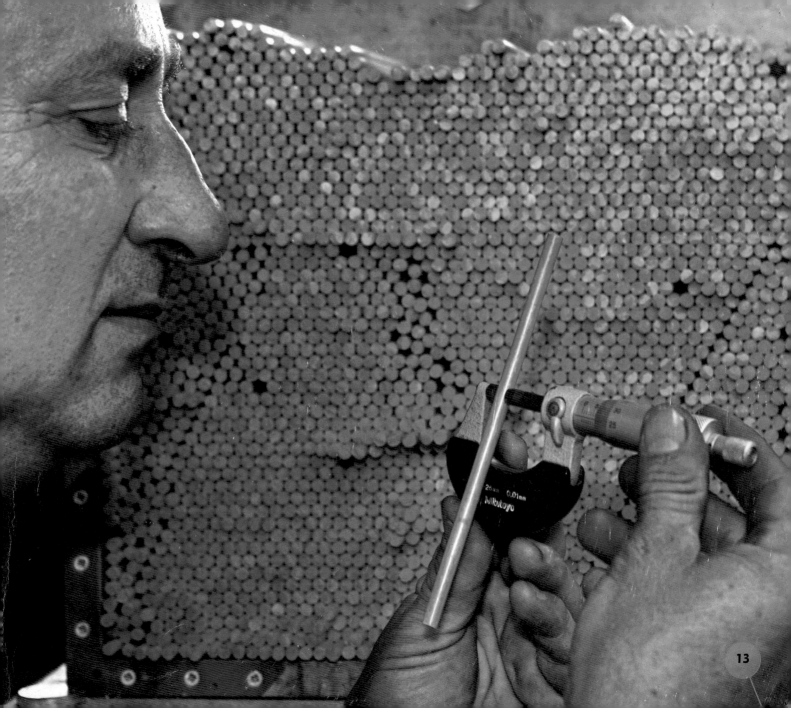

A machine wraps the crayons.

The crayons are sent into a machine that spins. It wraps each crayon in a piece of paper. The paper is called a **label**. The label tells the name of the crayon's color.

A machine sorts the crayons.

Crayons of the same color line up in
the slots of a sorting machine. The
machine sorts the crayons into sets.
A set has crayons of different colors.

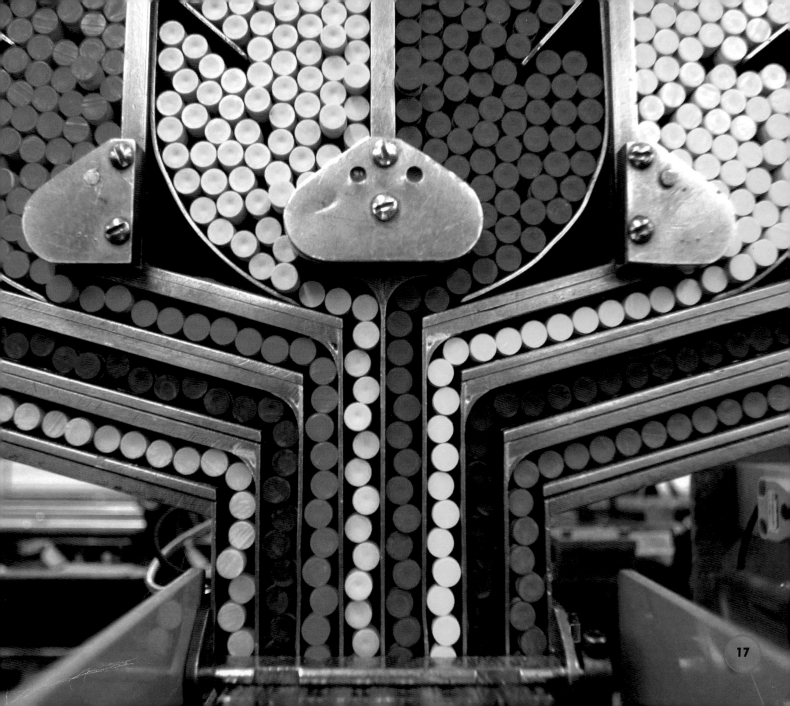

The crayons are boxed.

A packing machine puts the sets into boxes. Some boxes have just a few crayons. Some boxes have crayons of every color the factory makes.

The crayons are sent to stores.

A worker fills large cartons with boxes of crayons. The cartons are packed onto a truck. The truck takes the crayons to stores.

I draw pictures with many colors!

People buy crayons at the store. My crayon box has many colors. What should I draw?

Glossary

factory (FAK-tuh-ree): a building where things are made

label (LAY-buhl): a paper that names a crayon's color

mold (MOHLD): a container that shapes crayons

pigment (PIHG-mehnt): a powder that colors wax

vats (VATS): pots for melting wax

Index

LERNER
e
SOURCE

Expand learning beyond the printed book. Download free, complementary educational resources for this book from our website, www.lerneresource.com.